THE GIFT IS IN THE GIVING

True Christmas stories that will thrill and inspire you

BILL ARIENTI

Published by KHARIS PUBLISHING, imprint of
KHARIS MEDIA LLC

Copyright © 2016 Bill Arienti

ISBN: 10: 0-9971176-3-X
ISBN-13: 978-0-9971176-3-9

All KHARIS PUBLISHING products are available at special
quantity discounts for bulk purchase for sales promotions,
premiums, fund-raising, and educational needs. For details, write:

Kharis Media LLC
709 SW Elmside Drive
Bentonville,
AR 72712
Tel: 1-479-903-8160
info@kharispublishing.com
www.kharispublishing.com

Bill's stories continue to touch my heart and show the real meaning of what life is about. I'll find myself tearing up but then laughing a few minutes later. These beautiful and entertaining stories tug at my heart strings. Thank you Bill for the wonderful life experiences that you share with us through your gift of writing.

Andrea Daiute-Sweet
Massachusetts

While reading the "Gift is in the Giving," all I could think about was how genuinely captivating the author managed to make true life stories to read like fiction. Not only did he hold my attention from beginning to end, but he touched a myriad of emotions. Bill brings life to real life. He gives hope through insight. He writes with unbridled honesty and humor. He touches the spirit and soul of his reader.

Nuncy DeLeo Sullivan
Massachusetts

Nowadays, it is a sad fact of life that too often we rush through our days, spending more time staring at screens than looking into the faces of those around us. Additionally, what is most unfortunate is for many, Christmas has lost its joy and wonder. It seems it's just the time of year when the "to do" list seems to get longer, and the days feel more manic than they do festive.

Bill's wonderful book is an interesting and touching reminder of what Christmas should be. Detailing true stories from his remarkable life, Bill shows us all how important it is to live our lives with an open heart and to pay attention to our fellow travelers on this sometimes weary road of life. We all have gifts to give - our time, patience, understanding, empathy, acknowledgment. This book is a lovely reminder of how precious those gifts are.

Lisa Greco
Texas

DEDICATION

For my parents,

Charlie and Theresa

For their love, their guidance and their compassion.

CONTENTS

FORWARD

November 1, the day after Halloween, it all begins. Displays of candy and costumes are replaced with Christmas trees, ornaments and colorful wrapping paper in every store. Radio channels begin their cavalcade of Christmas music, and Sunday newspapers are filled with ads displaying this year's newest and must-have items. Christmas, it seems, is no longer a time of peace on earth and goodwill towards men, but rather a marketing gimmick used to boost sales for stores, often transforming a year of losses into a tidy little profit for their owners and stockholders.

It wasn't always this way. As a matter of fact, from the many stories that I have heard, Christmases past were less of expectation, and more of innovation and inspiration. As the generation most immediately preceding mine lived through the years of the Great Depression, their experiences were almost the opposite of what we today take as commonplace. If gifts were given, they were very inexpensive and usually only one toy or game, if any, per family, no matter how many children. A special meal, a few pieces of candy, some nuts and fruit in their stockings. It was a time when receiving material objects paled in comparison to the intimacy of a family gathering together in an atmosphere of love and togetherness that made Christmas special.

Although the act of exchanging gifts has overshadowed the sense of family and togetherness, there are still those who maintain the importance of love, sharing and togetherness as the cornerstone of the holiday. There still are families who realize that great riches can be amassed by selflessly giving of themselves to others than could ever be achieved by receiving. The knowledge that your actions have made an actual difference in some less fortunate person's life is a gift to you that cannot be wrapped, cannot be bought, but most certainly can be used the whole year through. It is a feeling that can make the darkest day bright and offer you warmth on the coldest day.

In my life, for reasons not known to me, I have been the recipient of this type of gift on a number of occasions. I cannot say it is from my devout religious practices, which are for all intents and purposes non-existent; nor can I attribute them to my virtuous actions throughout the year, because, in all honesty, I am far from angelic. Whatever the reason, I thank the powers that brought these wonderful and heartfelt experiences into my life with everlasting gratitude.

With the exception of some name changes for the sake of privacy, all the stories you are about to read are absolutely true. There are no exaggerations or poetic license taken. They are as precisely written as they could possibly be to illustrate each event, and each one gives me great joy, pleasure and comfort when I reminisce. Each person in these stories have in some way changed my life for the better. They have given me gifts of compassion, wisdom, generosity, happiness, patience and satisfaction. There is no Christmas tree in the world big enough under which these precious gifts would fit. There is not enough wrapping paper and tape in the world to cover their enormity. My finances may be quite modest, but my soul is rich beyond compare because of these people and these events.

I hope you enjoy reading these stories with as much passion as I enjoyed in writing them. I did not look for these situations, they just happened to be blessed upon me. In actuality, they could very well have happened to you, and still can; all you have to do is be open and willing to help. I promise you that the excitement and happiness of being part of events like these brings will give you a feeling of spiritual jubilation to which no other gift that you have ever received could ever compare. Merry Christmas

CHAPTER 1

1992

It was a number of years ago that my wife
and I took our nine year old son Mark and his
friend to a screening of the movie *The Polar
Express*. The movie tells the story of a young
boy whose belief in Santa Claus is waning as
he matures into adolescence. However,
through the miracle of Christmas, he is given
the gift of belief in Santa Claus, and this belief
is manifested in his ability to hear the sound
of Santa's sleigh bells that are inaudible to all
other non-believers. The movie was as
thrilling as the book and is filled with
breathtaking animation and enchanting music.
Even as an adult, I loved it!

On the way to the theater, I asked my son's
friend what he hoped Santa Claus was going

to bring him. He replied by telling us he no longer believed in Santa because he saw the things he wanted for Christmas under his mother's bed. My son, who still believed in Santa, then asked me directly, "Dad, is Santa Claus real?"

This was one of the questions I had been dreading. I knew that if I told the absolute truth, an aspect of my son's childhood would forever be lost, but I could not give a canned answer either as his friend would surely question any statement I made. So instead, I decided to tell him a story of my experiences, which I hoped would quell the question for some time.

When I was eight years old, close to Christmas, my father took me to a local toy store. As we walked in, he told me to go pick out four toys a boy my age would like. I asked him if they were for me, and he responded that they were for some children who had much less than I could imagine. I did what my father asked me and he bought the toys. We then got into his car and drove to a place I had never been before. I asked him where we were, and he told me it was a place for kids without parents, an orphanage called the Home for Little Wanderers.

As we walked in, a woman met us at the

door. My father and I handed her the gifts and she thanked us. She took the gifts, turned and closed the door. I looked into my father's eyes and saw his look of contentment, but I was a little less thrilled. As he saw my somewhat disappointed face, he asked me what the problem was. I told him that I wanted to see the orphans, that I wanted to see the look on their faces when they received what I thought were really cool gifts. He then told me something that has stayed with me ever since: "The gift is in the giving." It was then, for the first time in my life that I actually heard the bells of Santa's sleigh.

Annually, for the following ten years my father and I retraced our steps and made our Christmas pilgrimage to the Home for Little Wanderers. It was a trip that I looked forward to and cherished. Then, when I was 18, my father became very ill. We knew this would be the last Christmas we would share together, and his illness made it impossible for him to do the thing we loved so much. That year the smiles on our faces were forced, and the laughter was purely fabricated. That Christmas was more reflective than joyous, more somber than festive. I still heard the sleigh bells, but they were not as loud and clear as I had become accustomed. We made it through

Christmas, and my father died a few months later.

The following Christmas season was difficult for us all. My mother, who was always so proud of her colossal and festively-decorated Christmas tree decided not to decorate our home. My family gathered to exchange gifts and have dinner, but there was no Christmas music, and with the exception of a few Christmas cards positioned around the house, no one would have ever known what we were celebrating.

As I now reminisce, a lone trip to the toy store and to the Home for Little Wanderers would most likely have shattered the melancholy mood I was in and flooded me with the feelings I so loved; however, I just could not bring myself to do it. I felt that it was not my trip, but our trip, and making it alone would never be the same. The symphony of sleigh bells in which I once reveled for the first time in many years was silent. Christmas was now just another day. Buying gifts was more of a chore than a celebration, and exchanging gifts was just that.

Years passed as they will, and I followed in my father's footsteps and became a firefighter. Christmases were as ordinary as every other holiday. Long gone were the sound of bells and excitement and revelry I once associated with this holiday. Although I missed it dearly, I now went by the adage that Christmas was for children.

One specific year I had been very fortunate financially and decided it was only right to share my blessings and help someone less fortunate. I decided to go into the South Boston Postal Annex, where I had read in the newspapers about families that send letters to Santa Claus. I took a stack of letters from Quincy and began to read through them. In these letters were not the everyday requests for toys from children, but rather things people in my situation take for commonplace. The letters were heart-rending, as children asked not for bikes and video games, but rather for warm coats for themselves and their mothers, pajamas and blankets. I was so moved by these requests that I felt sad to only take three letters of wishes to fulfill.

As I left the Annex and began shopping, a familiar sound began to once again fill my head. Although faint and somewhat muffled, it was surely distinguishable — sleigh bells. I felt a smile on my face that I had not felt since I was a child. This again was Christmas. This again was the feeling that my father instilled in me, that the gift was in the giving. I shopped and bought everything on each list, and then went further, hoping the toys I was buying were suitable for each person in the letter. With each bag I placed into the back of my truck the clarity of the sound became more and more precise.

I took the packages home, wrapped each one with my wife and called the families who sent the letters. I planned to drop off the gifts to each family on Friday, December 19. On that morning, when I packed my car and began my task, sleigh bells were ringing and the cold biting air was as refreshing as a day in early autumn. However, this glorious feeling was short-lived. Upon reaching the homes of those who had sent the letters, it was evident that these were not people who were in such desperate need as had been portrayed. In these apartments were people who had better furnishings than I ever thought of owning — leather furniture, new televisions and sound systems. Wrapped gifts were already under the Christmas tree as I stood there in the doorway with four trash bags filled with presents. Of the thousands of truly needy people who sent those letters, I had had the misfortune of choosing the three families who played the system for everything they could get. As I left each apartment with hardly a thank you, the sound of the bells was gone for what I was sure would be forever.

The next day I went to work at the fire department dispatch office. I told the story to my brother firefighters, and they could see how disgusted I was with humanity. And then it happened. The phone rang a hundred times earlier that day. It could have rung the day before, but it didn't. Anyone could have answered it, but they didn't. Whether it was dumb luck or divine intervention I will never know, but that phone call was about to change my life.

As I answered the phone with "Quincy Fire Department, how can I help you," a woman's voice came on the receiver and asked if I was a firefighter. I said yes and the woman first apologized for what she was about to say but then continued and told me that all her six year old son wanted for Christmas was a fire truck, and she could not afford to buy him one. She asked me if I could help.

With my experiences I was somewhat hardened, but I could not refuse. I took her address and told her I would bring one the next morning, Sunday. I was kicking myself for being such a soft touch, but I always found it hard to refuse anyone help. So after work I went to the local department store and bought a fairly inexpensive fire truck. I brought it home, wrapped it and placed it on the table near my front door. The next morning my wife gave me a small shopping list to fill while I was out. I took the gift and drove to the address the woman had given me, an apartment house known for a less than desirable element. I rang the front doorbell and went in. I found her apartment, knocked on the door, and was greeted by a petite, demure woman. She greeted me warmly and invited me in.

As I entered the apartment I observed that the only furnishings were a small kitchen table with two chairs, a full size mattress on the floor in the living room, and a crib next to it. She called her son into the kitchen, telling him a firefighter had something for him. The young boy came into the kitchen, I handed him the gift, and the boy looked into my eyes and thanked me. He took the gift, went back into the living room, placed the gift in the corner and resumed playing with his baby sister.

The woman offered me a seat and told me she would love to offer me something to eat or drink. She then opened the refrigerator to show that all she had was half-gallon of milk and a loaf of bread. She told me that she had just left her physically abusive husband in Connecticut with only the most basic of needs, hoping he would not find them. I told her that I had to leave, but would be back shortly with a little help. She again thanked me, and her son came to the door and asked me if I was a real firefighter. I told him I was, smiled, and left.

I drove to a store owned by my friend Chris. I told him the whole story and asked him if he would match me dollar for dollar while I bought these people some food. He told me to go get a box and fill it up, then bring it up to him. He then asked me if my truck was in the parking lot. I filled a large box as he had asked and brought it to him. He told me to give him ten dollars and we would be even. I smiled, hugged him and wished him a merry Christmas. When I went to my truck I saw that he had placed another three boxes of goods in the back of it along with a Christmas tree. I put the box into my truck with the rest of the items and drove back to the apartment.

Upon reaching the apartment house, I rang the doorbell and told the woman I had something for her. I then carried the four boxes of food up to her apartment along with the Christmas tree. As I brought the boxes in, she thanked me and cried. Her son was as excited as a young boy could be, and with each box I carried, once again the sound of sleigh bells began to reappear. When all the items along with the tree were in the apartment, I wished them a merry Christmas and left. They stood at the door, the mother crying and wishing me well, the son jumping up and down shouting merry Christmas.

When I reached my truck I wiped away my tears, took a deep breath and reached into my pocket for my keys, where I found the shopping list my wife had given me. I drove back to Chris's store and walked in. He looked at me and shook his head. "You are not going to believe this," he said. ""God must have sent you!"

"Close," I replied. "My wife did."

Chris told me that a number of people had heard the story of this family and began giving him money to get these people some gifts. He then handed me an envelope with four-hundred dollars and told me to go shopping for them. We looked at each other, both choking back tears and wished each other well. I bought the items on my wife's list and then went to the closest department store, where I bought enough gifts to fill the back of my small pickup truck.

I drove to the apartment building, used my fire department key to gain entrance to the building and quietly brought all the bags up to the apartment. When I finished bringing them up, I knocked on the door, ran down the stairs as fast as I could, and hid in the basement. I heard the door open and the woman's voice calling her son through her tears. As she cried I could hear her say, "Thank you, Jesus" and her son shouting, "Santa Claus came!" But most importantly, I could hear more profoundly than ever before the sound of the bells from Santa's sleigh, and it has stayed with me to this very day.

So, to my son Mark, you ask me if Santa Claus is real, and I can honestly say this. Santa might not always be a man, he might not have a white beard, and he may not wear a red suit, but as long as people truly care for each other and love is in their heart, even if it's only for this one special day, then I can say to you, without a doubt, that Santa Claus is as real as you and me.

CHAPTER 2

1998

Golfing is such a wonderful pastime. Taking a long walk on freshly cut grass, enjoying the beauty of nature around you, and spending time with friends all combine to create a great experience. However, there is one drawback: you have to hit that little white ball into a hole. As you can probably guess from that last sentence, I am not a very good golfer; but, this story isn't about golf. It's about bringing happiness to someone in a sad situation. It's a story that reveals the goodness of one very special man who has made it his life's work to help others. But most importantly, it's a tale that lets us know that when the feeling that all is lost comes crashing down upon us, somehow, someway the world will make things right.

Through my travels I had met two very

nice and extremely successful businessmen. Jack and Oakie worked in the investment industry, and performed their craft quite well. We met through business, but became very good friends. Unlike many people in this type of business, they were less concerned with their bottom line, but instead had a genuine concern with the well-being of their clients. Many Massachusetts public employees were investing with the company these men operated, and no matter who in the State that I asked, they all came to me offering their highest of recommendations. The two men showed me their product and what special options only they were offering. I compared them to the other companies that offered similar products, and found that there was no comparison. After all this work and research, I finally agreed to introduce them to my fellow city employees.

It was in the later part of the 1990s, before the big recession. Everyone was very happy with the way their investments were progressing, and credited their financial success to Jack and Oakie. To show their appreciation for my help, the two men offered me a number of gifts. Although very appreciative, I would not accept any of them for ethical reasons. In all honesty, I really didn't need any of the things that they presented to me, but I did thoroughly enjoy the friendship that was created with these two men, and we stayed close friends for a number of years.

One August day, Oakie called me with an invitation to play golf in a tournament they were running at a prestigious golf course in Sandwich. I chuckled as I asked him if he really wanted me on such a nice golf course. He answered with a resounding, "Yes, and do I have a surprise for you!" By now Oakie knew that I would not accept anything from his business, so I was puzzled what the surprise could be. "You're going to put a ringer on my team?" I probed. Oakie laughed. "Well, close," he replied. "When I say Boston Bruins, what name comes to mind?" Well, as a boy growing up in the 1960s and 1970s, I, like every other Massachusetts child, worshiped Boston's patron saint of hockey, Bobby Orr. "Bobby Orr is going to be there?" I asked with a lift in my voice. "Better than that, buddy, he is playing on our team!" Oakie replied.

Now, this takes some explanation. As revered as the names and feats of Bill Russell, Tom Brady, and Ted Williams are in the Boston sports world, they all live in the shadow of Boston's greatest sports legend, Bobby Orr. Orr came into the National Hockey League as a very young man with surprising talent; however, it wasn't long before that talent developed into superstardom. As a defenseman, he restructured the position as only he could, and brought it to a level of excellence. His speed on the ice allowed him to play offense in the opponent's zone like the most experienced center, yet get back on defense quick enough to overtake his opponents and help protect his goalie. His shots were as precise as that of the most accurate sniper, and his passes seemed to never miss his teammate's stick. Every boy had a replica of his shirt, complete with the big number four on the back, and his poster was taped to their bedroom wall.

In the final game of the 1970 Stanley Cup Championship, Orr, taking a pass from his good friend Derek Sanderson from behind the net, gracefully tipped the spinning puck into the net behind the goalie for the sudden-death win in overtime. But what came next is what made him immortal. The stick of one of his opponents found its way into the blades of Orr's skates. The opponent raised his stick at the exact moment that Orr had jumped in excitement. Orr's body went from a vertical jump to a horizontal soar which was captured in one of the greatest sport pictures of all times. The world now knew what Boston fans had known all along, Bobby Orr could fly!

As good—no—as *spectacular* as Orr was playing hockey, those skills paled in comparison to the absolute kindness and goodness of this man. Being the victim of an unscrupulous agent, Orr lost all of his earnings that he had made over his professional career. As this might have crushed other men, it was just another experience, another challenge this man lived through and overcame. Even though his situation was tentative at best, whenever he saw his friends in dire situations, he would dedicate his life to ensure their health, safety and happiness. His signature, although as valuable as gold to many hockey fans, in the collector's market, it is virtually worthless. This is not because he was not considered a giant of the sports world, but because his autograph was so abundant. Unlike other sports greats, he never charged for his autograph, and never refused anyone who asked for it. In a time that we try to encourage our children not to consider sports celebrities as heroes, Bobby Orr stands apart; he was, is, and will always be my hero.

Being an adult in my thirties and a professional firefighter, I am expected not to react to surprising announcements, and I have always been pretty good at it, but this time I had all I could to hold in my excitement and maintain a sense of professional decorum. "Oh, great!" I said, about three octaves higher than my normal voice, but inside I was doing the Snoopy happy dance. I had met Orr a few times before at different events, but this time I was his golf partner for 18 holes! A whole day spent with my hero — somebody pinch me!

The golf tournament was epic. Although I got to play with Orr, other notable Bruin players from their heyday were there as well, such as Derek Sanderson, Gerry Cheevers, Johnny McKenzie, Ken Hodge, and more recent Bruins alumni, including Cam Neely, Ray Bourque and Chris Nilan. It was like the Mount Olympus for hockey fans. Upon arrival, all participants received a Bruins baseball hat, a wooden hockey stick and a Sharpie pen. The players were more than happy to sign each of the items with the Sharpie. The fact that I lost a dozen balls and played my most horrible game of golf in my life was of no consequence, as I got to play that round with my hero.

***

Smoke billowed from the second floor windows as flames pushed out the windows on the first floor below. Immediately upon viewing the scene from down the street, the responding officer transmitted over the radio on the fire engine, "Quincy Engine two to fire alarm, we have heavy smoke and fire showing, strike the second alarm." The first fire truck had not yet even reached its destination, but it was unknown if people were still inside the building, and he was not taking any chances. Once on scene, the officer found the occupants of the house standing outside in the frigid weather and asked if anyone was still inside. To his relief, a woman, obviously and understandably upset, answered no. She informed the officer that everyone, as well as the pets, were accounted for. This information gave the responding firefighters sufficient information to employ the tactics necessary to battle this fire.

"All occupants are out of the building; I repeat, all occupants are out of the building!" called the officer over his radio, notifying all other incoming apparatus of the situation. "Have the next due engine drop us a line."

As the sound of the engine of the apparatus got louder, the long canvas covered hose expanded as water coursed through it. The crowd, gathering in the below freezing temperature, watched as the officer and one other man put their masks on their faces, their helmet atop their heads, and grabbed the now full hose line. Their hands protected in heavy leather gloves, lifted the weighty, charged hose by the nozzle and made their way inside the burning house. Shortly after Engine 2 arrived, a longer style fire truck pulled up and parked directly in front of the house. The emblem, Quincy Ladder 5, was emblazoned across its side as well as on the side of the hydraulic aerial ladder that laid on top of the truck.

As they parked the ladder, the three men jumped out and immediately, without a word to one another, performed specific tasks in unison. It was a synchronized performance as the three firefighters worked flawlessly in their process to operate the heavy aerial. As one man climbed atop the ladder truck, the sound of the powerful engine began to build in intensity all the way up to a mighty roar. A moment later the enormous metal structure slowly ascended from its horizontal position, and as it rose, it turned towards the building on fire. The other two men donned their heavy protective gear, put on their air tanks and took a large orange circular saw from a compartment on the truck. Once the operator got the aerial pointed in the proper direction, he pushed a lever and the ladder quickly extended, further and further until it reached the roof. The two other men raced up the steel rungs without any concern for their own well-being. When they reached the very tip of the ladder they leaped, one at a time, as gracefully as they could onto the slanted roof, never for an instant losing their balance. More engines arrived and the firefighters performed the additional duties necessary to combat the intense flames. As the water flowed from the engines, hose couplings and hydrants, the frigid temperatures instantly turned it into ice the moment it touched the ground, causing an invisible glaze over the asphalt street and sidewalk. The firefighters on the roof had cut a large hole from which tremendous plumes of black smoke were billowing. Other firefighters did their strenuous jobs, now made even more difficult as they were slipping on the treacherously dangerous iced over ground.

After what seemed like an eternity to those

watching from across the street, the fire was finally out. The once black smoke had turned to white steam, and the house that was brown before the fire started was now covered in an opaque layer of inch thick ice. Although the structure of the house was saved by the efforts of the firefighters, the belongings inside were completely destroyed. What made this even more upsetting was that this was the week before Christmas. The gifts that had been wrapped in bright colored paper were now just big piles of wet lumpy cardboard. The tree that was painstakingly adorned with the family's traditional ornaments collected throughout the years was now just one long trunk, barren of any needles. Just the melted wires of Christmas lights that encircled the bare branches. As much as firefighters expel every ounce of energy to fight every fire to which they respond, the knowledge that their efforts are the only thing that could save a Christmas for a young family gives them just a little more grit to get the job done even faster. Conversely, if we cannot save that Christmas, the feeling of despair we feel for the family suffering such a loss is profound.

***

The newspaper laid on the floor of my front porch, folded tightly into itself. As I opened my front door to retrieve it, the cold wind snatched the door from my hand and opened it widely. It was freezing out. I closed the door, took the newspaper inside and unfolded it. Picking up my coffee, I turned the paper onto its front page to the black and white pictures of flames devouring a big house. "Quincy house fire leaves 5 homeless" read the bold headline over the picture. As I sat and read the entire article I could not help but feel a sense of empathy. The reporter told the story of how two parents had to explain to their children that everything that they owned, every birthday present they had been given, every treasure or keepsake that they saved had been destroyed by the fire. As Quincy Firefighters, we understand how important we are to the community in which we serve, and we also know just how important the community we serve is to us. We often sponsor a number of sport teams, donate to numerous charities and help out members of our community in need, all with money gathered directly from our personal accounts. Never was there a family more in need than this family. As secretary of the Firefighters Union, I awaited a call from its president, Jim

McCarthy. Jimmy was a very kind man who always thought of others. Like clockwork, a few minutes later the phone rang; it was Jimmy. He informed me that he devised a plan. We would open a savings account at the local credit union to which people could donate, if they were so inclined. We would then find out what the children wanted for Christmas, hoping that maybe we could take some of the pain away from the family by replacing the now destroyed gifts. Once agreed, we began to put our plan in motion. It was Jimmy's job to approach the family and create a list of the children's wishes.

After finding the location of the now homeless family, he called them and asked the mother if he could come by for a few minutes. It was fortunate that the children were in school that morning, so they could talk freely inside the hotel room. When the mother heard our intentions her emotions erupted into a flood of tears. "I can't ask you to do this, thank you so much though," she said to Jimmy through her tears. Jimmy told us that he took her hand in his and said, "You didn't ask us to do this, and it is already done. The money has already been allocated and the firefighters are just waiting for the list to go shopping. This is how we show our thanks and appreciation to our community." Jimmy took out a notebook as she composed herself. She began to rattle off a number of toys and games for which the children had asked, punctuating each item with "Thank you so much." When she had finished, he asked the children's sizes. Shaking her head she informed Jimmy what size each child wore. He then asked her what size she and her husband were, which again brought her emotions to the forefront. "No, No, please, just the children is more than enough." Jimmy shook his head, saying, "Please tell me your sizes or else we will just buy you clothes that don't fit." Hesitantly she told Jimmy her and her husband's sizes. "We cannot thank you enough," she said as Jimmy exited the hotel room. "They are delivering a trailer for us to live in tomorrow, and it will be right next to our house." Jimmy nodded and said "Okay, take care," and brought the list to those who had volunteered to do the shopping. His job was now complete.

Two days later the same reporter who covered the fire wrote a follow-up story. The story journaled how the family was coping, how the children were handling the situation, and how to donate if anyone wanted to help. However, out of the whole article, one line caught me by surprise more than any other part. The family's oldest son, twelve year old Doug, said in an interview that as much as he was upset about losing the house, he was also upset about losing his most valuable possession: a hockey stick signed by Bobby Orr. After reading the article, I called Jimmy and asked him if Doug's mother had mentioned a hockey stick. Jimmy said no, she never mentioned it. Of all the gifts and desires Doug's mother had asked for, she had never mentioned a hockey stick signed by Bobby Orr. I don't know if she forgot with all the turmoil or if she just thought it was too difficult a gift to acquire. I took a deep breath, and a smile emerged on my face.

The Quincy Firefighters had delivered the gifts we had purchased to the family on December 22. Having a hat signed by all the Bruins, I had no need for a stick as well. I didn't want to bother the family again, so instead I attached a big bow to the stick, and on Christmas Eve, on our way home from our annual family get together, I stopped by the house and placed the hockey stick on stairs of the trailer. I didn't knock or wait around to see the response, I just got back in my car with my wife and my son and drove away into the night.

I don't know what happened, and I don't care to know what happened. All I knew is that no matter how surprised, no matter how lucky he felt the moment he found that stick, his joy was just a fraction of the happiness that I received giving it to him. Quincy is my community. It is the city where I was born, educated, and spent my entire youth and adolescence. It is the city that employed my father, and took care of him, and in extension, us when he could no longer perform the duties of a firefighter. It was Quincy that then took care of my mother after his death. Although it is a fairly big city, the way people come together for someone in need makes it feel like a small town. I consider myself very fortunate to work for such a great community, and this was my way, as small as it was, to somehow pay them back.

CHAPTER 3

2001

They fell through the cracks. Five little words that more often than not denote a mistake that was made which has or eventually will cause someone an injustice or pain. It's a common excuse that is used in both public as well as private industry, and immediately takes the blame away from the guilty party. Those words of seething anger that are just waiting to be expelled by the affected party's mouth have just been neutralized by the utterance of this five word phrase. It immediately triggers a do over, a second chance to do the job correctly. Sometimes there is nothing that can rectify an incident where someone falls through the cracks, but this time, falling through the cracks brought love and happiness, wonder and joy to what otherwise would have been a chaotic event.

"I make the motion that we adopt five families for Christmas from the Germantown

Neighborhood Center," came a call from the crowd. "Second!" was immediately shouted by another. The old Navy hall was partially filled with a number of Quincy Firefighters. The department held their regular union meetings the third Thursday night of every month, and that night about forty firefighters were in attendance. "Motion made and seconded," stated Tommy Bowes from the head table. Tommy, the president of the Firefighters' Union, then asked the members in attendance, "Anything on the motion?", opening up the floor to discuss the proposal before them.

"On the motion," I shouted out as I raised my hand. "Go ahead Billy," ordered the president. "Mr. President, we have adopted families for the Germantown Neighborhood Center for a number of years now. Last year was a very difficult year for us, and the people of Quincy stood behind us in our fight. Since we have eight stations, let's adopt eight families. I think it's only fair to give as much as we can back to the people of Quincy." The hall was quiet. Tommy broke the silence by saying, "You're right Billy, does anyone want to make a motion to amend the motion to adopt eight families?" "Motion" came the call from the back of the hall; "Second" was again heard right after. "All in favor say aye, all opposed say nay; the ayes have it. Motion passed to adopt eight families." Tommy looked in my direction and smiled.

I had the pleasure of being Santa Claus's surrogate for the Firefighters' Union for a number of years. Some would say it was because of my jolly personality, others would argue it was for my rather rotund belly. Either way, playing Santa Claus was fun and always an enriching experience. There were three occasions each year when I would don the Union's Santa suit: the Quincy Firefighters Children's Christmas party; the Germantown Children's breakfast with Santa; and the night we delivered the gifts to the families that we adopted that year. Each of the events had its own perks, but my favorite was delivering the gifts. On December 23, a group of firefighters would take the spare fire engine we kept in storage and filled it with bags of wrapped gifts that we had purchased from the list of requests that each family had provided. We then wrapped the gifts in colorful papers and wrote the names on the gifts to identify whom it was for.

At dusk, we would all get on the truck and drive to the homes of the adoptive families. Our warning lights would illuminate the whole neighborhood, reflecting off the houses and buildings a hue of seasonal red. We would ring bells and sound the siren to complete the experience. Upon our arrival, children would race out of their homes shouting "Santa! Santa!" as they ran towards the truck. I would slowly exit the front seat dressed in red fur and white hair and beard. "Ho, ho, ho!" I would call out while standing on the running board of the engine. "Merry Christmas!" As I climbed down from the truck the children would gather in front of me while I handed out candy canes and handshakes. The excitement was palpable as each child knew Santa had specifically come to visit them.

***

This being the October Union meeting gave us more than adequate time to get the lists in hand, shop for each of the eight families, and get all the wrapping done. We each had our duties to perform in this annual endeavor, and with everyone's help it always came off without a hitch. A week after the meeting Tommy approached me with an envelope of papers. "Cathy asked me to thank you," Tommy said as he handed me the envelope. Cathy Quigley was God's emissary here on earth. She was the manager of the

Germantown Neighborhood Center, a community center in the public housing development in Quincy. Cathy had organized this center, and through her hard work and undying dedication, she grew it from a small closet-like room in the neighborhood elementary school all the way up to assuming the occupancy of a closed Catholic church. Her actions not only have brought joy and relief to so many, she has also saved the lives of a number of people who were at risk in a variety of dangers situations. She is a sweetheart, and a bully; an apologist, a defender as well as a persecutor. She is a warm hug and a swift kick in the butt. What makes her amazing is she can be all these things all within the same discussion. She is a woman like no other, a woman you cannot refuse, and a woman that you cannot help but love.

Our relationship began a number of years earlier when I was president of the Quincy Firefighters. She had just taken over the center and contacted me to ask for assistance in their Christmas drive. I told her that I would discuss it with the members of my union, but I was sure that we would be able to do something to help out.

As fate would have it, about an hour later

my phone rang again. This time it was a representative from Regan Public Relations Company that worked for Dunkin' Donuts. The woman informed me that Dunkin' Donuts would like to help out the Fire Department around Christmas time. They wanted to show their appreciation for our service to the citizens of Quincy by offering meals or other gifts. "It's funny that you're calling me today," I chuckled as I quickly devised a plan in my head. "The firefighters are all set, but thank you nonetheless for your concern and generosity. However, I did receive a call this morning from an organization in the city that helps less fortunate families. Would you be interested in possibly combining our abilities and doing a joint venture to help them?" The woman could not contain her excitement of the proposition. "Tha — that would be fantastic!" she said with nothing less than a jubilant lift in her voice. This was much more than she had ever expected. "We would be honored to participate in something like that!" Smiling on the inside as much as the outside, I told the woman that I would set up a meeting with all the appropriate parties, and that together we would create a memorable event. Within a few minutes a meeting was scheduled for the following week.

The tiny room was filled to capacity. Along with Cathy and me, there were two representatives from Regan Public Relations, as well as Victor and Octavio, the Dunkin' Donuts franchises owners. We sat on children's school chairs around a semi-circular table and after introductions we began to brainstorm on how we could best help the community. About two hours later, our legs and feet aching from lack of circulation as a result of sitting on the small chairs, we were finished. That day we had put together a plan that would last for fifteen years. The first week of December, the Quincy Firefighters would run a toy drive outside the local department store, and Dunkin' Donuts would provide refreshments for the firefighters. The second week of December, Dunkin' Donuts would hold an event called Breakfast with Santa, and the Quincy Firefighters would assist by providing Santa and a number of firefighter volunteers for assistance. Then the night of December 23, the Quincy Firefighters would present the gifts to the families that we adopted for the holidays.

With our plan set, we would kick off the endeavor with a press and photo opportunity with Quincy resident, and then soon to be national celebrity comedian, Steve Sweeny. As we stood inside the Dunkin' Donuts, lined up and awaiting the photographer, Cathy looked at me and whispered, "Do you think we bit off more than we can chew?" I smiled at her and laughed, "Like I always say Cathy, go big or stay home." After a few more clicks accompanied with the obligatory flashes of bright lights, the press session was complete and the plan was set in motion.

***

Christmas shopping is far from one of my favorite things to do. I have been known to go into a mall with a handful of cash and finish all my shopping in less than four hours. Any questionable gift ideas would be replaced by gift certificates at the recipient's favorite store (or at whatever store where I happened to end up when I decided that I was finished). So after receiving the lists, I asked Tommy what he had left to do that afternoon. He told me that he was done after this meeting. With the time being 12:30, I asked him if he wanted to go out for lunch; "It's on me" I explained. Tommy agreed, and I drove us to Pizzeria Uno fourteen miles away at the Hanover Mall. Now, to be honest, there were plenty of good restaurants in Quincy to have lunch, but if we ate at one of them, it would have been much easier for Tommy to get a ride home after I told him that we were going shopping.

After lunch, and a couple of celebratory indulgences, I told Tommy that I needed to stop at the mall for a few things. I told him of the new store that ha d just opened that I thought he would like. Tommy accompanied me into the mall, and I showed him the store. Once the store had been perused, I had him follow me to the large department store in the mall. I took a carriage, gave it to Tommy, then took a carriage for myself and told him my intentions. To say that he was not happy would be an understatement, but his choices were extremely limited, so the protest was quickly ended, and the shopping commenced. Two hours and five thousand dollars on my American Express card later, we emerged from the mall with enough full bags of toys, games and clothes to fill the back of my truck.

On the afternoon of the December Union meeting a line of tables were set up as firefighters, equipped with scissors, tape and pens began to wrap the colossal pile of gifts. For the sake of full disclosure, our wrapping abilities were not up to the standard of stores like Macy's and Neiman/Marcus. In all honesty, it was not even as good as your local butcher wrapping an awkward shaped steak in white paper. But knowing what was beneath the wrapping would bring unbridled joy to young families of modest means, and honestly, wasn't that all that really mattered?

Once we were done, we brought the gifts into the spare room. We separated the packages into separate piles which corresponded with the eight families wish lists. As we brought the bags into the dark room, we noticed a large pile of toys in the corner. "Where did these come from?" I asked Tommy. He looked to where I was pointing and explained that they were from the Firefighter Children's Christmas party. "We always buy extra and a few families did not show up, so we can use them next year."

Finishing the wrapping by five o'clock gave us the opportunity to relax before the union meeting, so a short trek to Coops for pizza was in order. It was December 22, the day before the annual trip, and we were done. We began to tell stories of past firehouse Christmases and how we celebrated them with our second families. There were tales of the different meals that were prepared, the gift baskets dropped off from civic organizations as well as caring neighbors thanking us for our continued services. We also spoke of the hours spent yelling at each other, as together we attempted to assemble toys and bikes for our children. By the time seven o'clock rolled around, we were sufficiently fed and in a jolly, festive mood. We made our way to the monthly meeting where once our actions were discussed. The members of the Quincy Firefighters' Union thanked us for our work putting this event together, knowing that this would be appreciated by the community that served us so well over the year.

***

The streets were bare, and the temperature was 48 degrees. So far this had been a very mild winter. With the home heating oil price increasing by the day, the warmer weather was a welcome condition. I had just picked up the Santa suit at the cleaners, and our annual tradition was about to commence. I drove to the fire station, painted my eye brows and mustache with white poster paint, rubbed my cheeks and tip of my nose with red rouge, and slipped into the suit. Once the beard, wig and hat went on, I was Santa! Upon seeing me all decked out in my disguise, the on duty firefighters began to laugh. As we joked about my appearance, the bright red lights began to shine through the windows of the fire station and against the yellow brick interior wall. "Well, here's my ride," I said as the large garage door slowly opened. On the apron of the fire station sat Quincy Engine 9, an older non-commissioned fire engine with bags of gifts that filled the bed of the truck that once held hundreds of feet of hose. Two cars followed closely behind the engine, and once I took my place on the truck, the procession to Germantown began. Firefighter Luis Ruiz drove the fire engine down the streets of Quincy as I rang the bell and waved to those pedestrians and cars we passed. Smiles from the people of Quincy lined our route as the feeling of good will towards all built up in all of our chests.

The caravan made its way down Palmer Street and stopped at the large, brick, church-like structure at the rotary (the building, once St. Boniface Church, had closed its doors a few years earlier. The building stayed vacant for a while, but through Cathy's persistence, it was acquired by the Germantown Neighborhood Center). As we drove into the front circular driveway, Cathy hurried down the stairs along with her co-worker Claire Brennan, another wonderful, caring, loving woman. "Santa's here!" laughed Cathy as she approached the engine. I stepped out of the engine and stepped into the open arms of this extraordinary woman. "Oh Santa, I love you!" said Cathy as she squeezed me tightly in her arms. "You're an angel Cathy, I love you too," I replied.

As Cathy let go, Claire immediately took her place. These were special people. People who could experience ultimate joy and devastating heartbreak within moments of each other without missing a step in providing services to those in need. These people not only did their jobs, but sacrificed their spare time to help out in the cause as well.

When the greetings were over, Cathy handed us a paper with the addresses of nine families. Looking at the list I told her that she must have given us the wrong list, we only had eight families. Cathy began to read the names of the people on our list, but the last name she read did not have a corresponding list of needs in the packet we received. "We have a problem Cathy, we didn't get anything for this family," I informed her. This was new territory for us — we never had a problem like this before. "How old are the kids?" I asked. Cathy looked at her notes and told me a nine year old girl and two seven year old twin boys. I remembered the pile of gifts left over from the Christmas party back at the office. I looked at Tommy and Kevin who were in one of the cars following us, and said "Go back to the office and get whatever toys we have there. At least we can give them something," I instructed. "Great idea," said Tommy, "we'll be right back." The two got back into their car and raced out of the driveway and down into the darkness of Palmer   Street.

Turning to Claire, Cathy asked, "Do we still have that bag of clothes Sears donated?" Cathy looked pensive, bit her tongue, and said "Yes, I think we do, I'll go see," as she ran back into the building and down to the basement. A few minutes later she appeared with three large bags of clothes from Sears. The two ladies started digging through the bags and found a few articles of clothing that matched the sizes of the three children. Claire then ran into the adjoining room and returned with an armful of tissue paper and gift bags. Together they wrapped the clothes in tissue paper and inserted them into individual gift bags. Then they wrote the names Denise, Alex and Stephen on the bags.

We decided to go out and deliver the packages to the other families while we waited for Tommy and Kevin. The thrill of being a surprise, coupled with the happiness one can only receive when they see the excitement in a child's eyes filled all of us with an incomparable sense of euphoria. Each of the families we had adopted were so grateful. Walking into their homes it was evident that they existed on the barest of essentials. Toys and clothes for the children brought them happiness, but toiletries, kitchen utensils, and food goods brought the parents a sense of relief. All in all, it's a feeling of joy one can feel only by being part of the experience.

When we had completed our route, we headed back to the church to load the gifts to that family who had fallen through the cracks. The gift bags were prepared beautifully, but the toys and games were wrapped as one can only imagine if they were wrapped by someone wearing boxing gloves. "I hope you don't do wallpapering for a second job," joked Luis as every box looked worse than the previous one. Fortunately firefighters have a good sense of humor and a very thick skin to absorb the barrage of insults hurled at them by their brother firefighters. We all got a good laugh, loaded the truck, and again we were on our way.

Fate is a very funny phenomenon. No one knows how or when it will affect us, it just does. More often than not we don't even know it's working upon us until the event is over and we can look back over the whole experience. In my life I have learned not to tempt fate, but rather to accept it, and hope that it is kind to me. I didn't always have this outlook, but after this night, it was ingrained into me with as much certainty and individuality as my own fingerprints.

The red lights sliced through the darkness on our way to Taffrail Road. It was getting late, so we dispensed with the bells and siren so as not to wake the children who were already asleep. We reached our final destination of the night to see a screen door holding back two small boys. On the exterior stairs in front of the door sat a girl with long brown hair. When I jumped out of the truck, the little girl darted over to us with reckless abandon. "Santa, Santa, Santa!" shouted the girl as she dashed across the concrete walkway. "Ho, ho, ho, merry Christmas Denise! My how you've gotten so much bigger since last year," I acknowledged as I walked towards the apartment house. Although this was my first time ever seeing the girl, I felt by saying those words I would offer some continuity from previous years.

Denise escorted me up the stairs where the

two little boys continued to peer out through the storm door without the slightest deviation. Denise opened the door for me and held it. "Alex, Stephen, merry Christmas! I can never tell the two of you apart, which one is Alex?" Denise extended her arm and identified the boy wearing the striped shirt was Stephen, and the boy wearing the pajama's was Alex. "Well everyone, stand back, the elves made you some gifts and gave them to the firefighters to help me deliver. Luis, Tommy, Kevin, Danny and Steve walked into the kitchen, all holding a bag or two. It was crowded in the small room, and with the warmer than normal temperature, wearing a wig, beard and fur suit was not in my best interest.

Suddenly, the boy's silence ended. "Santa, Santa, come here!" shouted the boys in unison. "Come see our Christmas tree!" ordered the boys as each one took one of my white gloved hands. Pulling me into the living room was very short lived, as once there, Stephen shouted "Come look at our stockings, Santa!" So off to the stockings the three of us went. "Our bedroom, our bedroom!" was the next location they wanted to drag me. Finally we made our way back to the living room. I sat on the couch with the three children and asked them to sing with me. When they said yes, I began: "You know Dasher and Dancer and Prancer and Vixen, Comet and Cupid and Donder and Blitzen; but do you recall, the most favorite reindeer of all..." The children took their cue perfectly, and joined in on the first words of the song, "Rudolph the Red Nosed Reindeer, had a very shiny nose..." The three children and I sung and swayed with the tempo, then the firefighters joined in and the whole house was immersed in song.

As we continued singing, I looked towards the entryway of the kitchen to see the silhouette of the children's mother crying — weeping at first, and evolving into a full sob. I sang louder to drown out the sounds of the woman's emotions as not to upset the children. After three songs, we began our exit from the house. The mother had composed herself enough to wish us well as we left her home. She shook our hands and thanked every one of us. When I reached the kitchen, I put my arm around the mother's shoulders, and gave her a hug from the side. "Merry Christmas," I said to the woman as I held her. She could not answer. "Don't cry, we love doing this. This is the best part of Christmas to us. We have a lot of fun." The woman looked up at me, her eyes still full of the tears that had not yet made their way down her cheeks. She took in a deep breath, blew it out, and staring me right in the eyes began to speak in a soft, strained voice. "You don't understand. Your gifts, they are all lovely, and thank you for all of them, but it's my kids." Her kids? With all we just went through for this woman she was now insinuating that we didn't get enough for her kids? "Your kids? What about them?" I asked. She again took in a deep breath, "Stephen and Alex were born with autism; they are almost eight years old, and they haven't said anywhere remotely close to the amount of words in their lifetime as they have said tonight. And never have I heard them sing," said the mother. "I don't know who you are, but thank you!"

Tears are not only a product of the weak, for at that moment it was my eyes that began to fill with water. I tried to say don't worry, or that's nice, or even wonderful, but when I opened my mouth, the only thing that came out were squeaks. I couldn't speak, the lump in my throat was obstructing my airway, making it even difficult to breath. With sweat flowing down my face, an uncomfortable lump in my throat and the inability to speak, I reached around the woman, hugged her close, and briskly left the house, ringing a few of the jingle bells I had around my wrist to replace my traditional "Ho, Ho, Ho!" Taking deep breaths all the way to the truck, I jumped in, turned my back to the home, and released my emotions with deep sobbing tears. It hurt so much, but felt so good.

CHAPTER 4

2014

It was a joyous Thanksgiving. My wife and I hosted my immediate family as well as some cousins to a festive celebration where no one wanted for anything. As we sat down for dinner, the twenty-four of us sat at long line of interconnected tables. After giving thanks for all of our blessings of health, family and comfort, we enjoyed our turkey, garnishes, fruit and lots of pies, cookies and a collection of other confections. Sitting on couches and easy chairs, bellies stuffed past a level of acceptance, the group of us reveled in stories of holidays past, reminiscing on how fortunate our lives are to have such a close loving family.

***

He sat beside his mother in an oversized chair. His head down with thumbs working feverishly on his electronic game. He ignored his mother's continued requests to lift his head and look at the television. On the flat screen hanging on the wall were colorful floats, bands and dancers as they passed by the front door of Macy's in New York City. The less than average number of people who sat in the waiting room with a multitude of ailments noticed the little boy perfectly content, sitting in his own little world while his mother seemed to be acting overly attentive. When his name was finally called, the mother took in a deep breath as she stood. She reached down to her right and lifted a large gym bag type satchel. From the way she lifted the bag, it seemed to be full. Together they walked through the door from whence the call came.

The mother and child joined a woman dressed in hospital scrubs in a small room that barely contained a small counter with a computer, two chairs, an upper cabinet and a blood pressure machine. "What's wrong today, Ronald?" asked the triage nurse as she kneeled down to Ronald's eye level. Ronald kept his head down, more interested in his electronic game than what was occurring around him. "Nothing," said Ronald in a soft, unassuming voice. Ronald, a boy no more than ten years of age was quiet, but not overly so. He stood about five feet tall, and his dark skinned face and hair had looked like they had not been washed recently.

"He poses a threat to himself and to others." Those words—those exact clinical terms used almost solely by healthcare professionals—flowed without trepidation from the boy's mother's lips. The triage nurse looked up quizzically. "Are you a nurse or P.A.?" said the nurse to the mother. "Nah, I work at Stop and Shop," replied the mother. "What makes you think he is a threat to himself and to others?" questioned the nurse with a tone of disbelief in her voice. "Ronald keeps getting in fights with my boyfriend's two daughters, and he's afraid for them," answered the Mother, "so he said Ronald needs to be put away." The nurse swallowed hard; she knew what this was. A quiet child, a fully packed garment bag, a new boyfriend in the house and a mother who knows the exact terms necessary with which to have someone committed. As a healthcare professional, it is vital that no matter how heartbreaking the incident, we must remain as stoic as possible. Having to accept an innocent little boy into her care knowing that this is nothing more than an abandonment tested every fiber of her being. The nurse's thoughts traveled to her family at home, working together as they prepared for a family Thanksgiving dinner for her while she spent her day at the hospital helping others. Never had she loved her family more and hated the outside world with the same intensity. The nurse wrote down the events as dictated by the mother, knowing deep down that these were merely manufactured events specifically to establish a reason for psychological internment.

Completing the examination, the nurse escorted the two into the pediatric emergency department and assigned Ronald to a private room with only a bed and a chair for furnishings. The nurse turned on the fluorescent light and told Ronald to make himself comfortable, and she would go get him a pair of pajamas. Upon returning to the room, the nurse gave Ronald the clean hospital pajamas, closed the door and went back to the nurse's station as quickly as possible to fume out of the sight of the boy and his mother. After a few minutes of decompression exercises the exhausted nurse summoned the hospital social worker.

At 10:00 a.m. the social worker and the

mother emerged from Ronald's room discussing the procedure. Kelly, the nurse who had absorbed all the emotion of the situation, watched as the two women walked by the nurse's station. As they reached the locked door, the social worker swiped her badge over the lock, opened the door and allowed the woman to exit. The social worker returned to talk with Kelly. Shaking her head, the social worker said "I think we are having the wrong one committed." Kelly agreed. "I have to call her when I can find a bed for him, she's going home to her boyfriend now for dinner. Happy Thanksgiving," mumbled the social worker as she walked out of the pediatric emergency room.

***

The day after a holiday always makes for a more difficult morning. Whether it be too much food, too much wine or just tired from all the work you put into it, the next morning is always better spent in bed. Unfortunately, that luxury did not apply to me that Friday morning, and as the sun slowly tore away the darkness in my bedroom, I rose to face another day of work. With schools closed for the long weekend it was a good bet that the emergency department would be inundated with younger patients in addition to the regular traffic that is seen on a daily basis.

With my stomach still full from the previous day's feast, I waddled into the ambulance garage that Friday morning. As we sat in the office awaiting the start of our shift, the EMS staff related the events of the previous day for each other's amusement. At five minutes to 9:00 we punched in, inspected our ambulances and called in to the dispatch office to notify them of our being in service. I had worked part time as an EMT at the hospital for about five years on the days that I was not working at the fire station to supplement my income. Immediately upon us signing on, dispatch called on the radio, "Ambulance five, A5, you have a transport from the pediatric emergency department to the Children's Home upon your arrival at the hospital." Pediatric patients being transported for any reason by an ambulance present additional challenges for the EMT, depending on the age, size, primary complaint, as well as specialized equipment that may be necessary. We acknowledged receiving the call and made our way to the hospital.

At 9:30 a.m. the pediatric emergency department was frantic. Every bed in every room was occupied. Additional beds and hospital cribs were placed in the locked units hallways to accommodate the overflow of ailing children. "Who are you here for?" asked Cheryl, a middle aged and well-seasoned charge nurse as we rolled our stretcher into the unit. My partner of the day, Al, looked down on a small piece of paper he held in his hand and read the name aloud, "Ronald Davis." Cheryl took a deep breath and sighed during her exhalation. "This is a tough one," the concerned nurse informed us. "His mother dropped him off Thanksgiving morning and left him here because, and I quote, he poses a threat to himself and to others." At the comment all three of us took a deep breath in through our noses and our eyes rolled back into our heads. We all heard this before; it was too perfectly said by someone not familiar with emergency medicine. "He's right there in room eight."

Al sat at the nurse's station and began to complete the paperwork necessary to transport this child. I made my way over to room 8 to see the door open, a television stand that was just outside the door. In front of the television stood a boy in New England Patriots pajamas silently watching a recording of *Shrek*. I walked over to the room and greeted Ronald, but he remained silent. "I love this movie. My favorite is Donkey," I said in an attempt to break the ice. Again, my words returned nothing to me but silence. Undaunted, I continued to try and elicit some type of verbal response from this boy. After mentioning the Patriots, Red Sox, Celtics, Bruins, race cars, soccer, and Disney, I got my first response from Ronald was when I mentioned his stuffed toy puppy. "I like dogs. His name is Courage." His voice was soft and clear. I had finally broken through. It took me ten minutes of chattering, but I finally got past the first gate. "He looks just like my dog," I said as I took out my phone and pulled up a picture of my golden lab Zeus. I gave Ronald my phone and he looked at the image of Zeus. When the screen went black he handed the phone back to me, looked up into my eyes through his black rimmed glasses and smiled. "He's funny," said Ronald.

That was my way in. Zeus and his antics would be the vehicle to bring this boy and me together. We went back into the room and chatted for a few minutes. He was a very intelligent boy with an exceptional vocabulary. During one small lull in the conversation I asked him to take my blood pressure. "I don't know how to do that" responded Ronald. "Well, let me show you how to do it, then you can do it, ok?" Ronald agreed, so I took his blood pressure and explained how and why we take it, then I gave him the machine and let him take mine. He laughed when I feigned injury and chuckled "You're silly!" I smiled back at him. Then, in an instant, the tone in his voice changed. "Is my mom coming back to get me?" Ronald said with an uncertainty in his voice that I had not heard from him before. "Let me go check," I answered, and I walked out of the room.

When I got to the nurses station, Al, without lifting his head, said "You're not going to believe this one." "What's going on?" I replied. "The mother got a new boyfriend who has two daughters that this kid doesn't get along with, so she just dropped him off, can you believe it? She dropped him off on Thanksgiving Day." I stepped back, and took a deep breath. "Is she coming back?" I asked on Ronald's behalf. Cheryl, standing right beside me, said "She told us that she will meet you over at the Children's Home at 11:30." I was as relieved as I was furious. What kind of person does something like this? How could you even consider yourself a parent if you are so readily willing to throw away your child? This call was going to require all the compassion and restraint that I could possibly muster inside me. "Is he ready to go?" asked Al, "I'm just about done here." "I'll go get him ready, does he know where he is going?" I inquired. "No, not yet" answered Al. With that I left the nurses station and returned to Ronald.

"Hey, big guy, do you want to get out of these pajamas and get dressed?" I said walking towards Ronald's room. "Yes, I'd like that" answered Ronald. I reached down and picked up his luggage. As I opened the zipper and looked into the bag I observed that the clothes were not only just rolled up and stuffed into the bag, but they were also all soiled, in need of a good laundering. Again, I said to myself how anyone could consider themselves a parent if they could do this to their child. I picked through his clothes in front of him, hiding my disgust, and selected the least dirty articles of clothing for this poor boy to wear. I pulled the curtain to offer Ronald privacy, and waited outside the room.

Al approached the room with his tablet and a white envelope in hand. "He ready?" asked Al. "In a minute," I answered. The sound of the metal hooks dragging across the aluminum pipe signaled us that Ronald was dressed. "Hi Ronald, I'm Al. I'll be riding in back with you, how you doo-in?" Al joked as he walked into the room. "Are we going to see my mom?" asked Ronald. "She is going to meet us at the Children's Home at 11:30," answered Al. Suddenly, I noticed Ronald's demeanor shift from what appeared to be a happy little boy to profound sadness. His gaze fell to the floor and tears began a trail from the corners of his eyes, down his cheeks and onto his dirty shirt. "I don't want to go back there," cried Ronald; "I'm not going." Ronald ran back into the room, jumped on his bed and pulled a blanket over his head. Al began to initiate a conversation with the upset boy, but found the same difficulties that I had encountered earlier. "Let me talk to him, Al," I requested. Al backed out of the room and I sat in the chair next to the bed. Silence recaptured the boy and held him tightly. He laid on the bed, and although I was merely inches away, he was alone. Face down, holding his stuffed dog, tears running under his black rimmed glasses and following down the contours of his face and into his pillow, Ronald again withdrew into a shell, but this one was much more rigid, and I would have to work much harder to penetrate it. "What's going on Ronald?" I whispered and leaned forward to maintain his privacy. No response was forthcoming. If this boy was going to be cooperative, I knew I was going to have to start from scratch again.

"How did Courage get his name?" I asked. Again, no response. "Is he named Courage after the Courage the dog cartoon? Do you watch that show? What is your favorite show?" My questions were returned with silence. I then asked if he knew the difference between bravery and courage... he looked up, still non-verbal, but any response was welcome at this point. I continued, "Bravery is when you have no fear. Courage is when you have fear, but overcome it to do what you have to do. Bravery can get you killed. Courage is what makes you a man."

"I'm not a man, I'm a little boy." Finally, words. I had once again broken through, but I knew I had to work fast and hard if I was going to keep Ronald from going back into his virtually impenetrable shell. "You may have the body of a little boy, but you are most definitely a man," I answered. "I know men ten times your age that don't have the courage that you have shown me here today."

"What courage did I show you?" With that, I got a conversation going. "You have been sitting in this room alone for two days. Did you cry? No. Did you make a fuss? NO! I know a lot of guys that would do nothing but hit the nurses buzzer all day asking if anyone called, or if he had visitors, or if someone could come in and scratch his butt." His pursed lips began to spread apart and turn up at the corners. I had a smile coming out of him. "You have no idea how itchy your butt gets when you get older. I'm scratching my butt all the time!" The tears detoured their way straight down his face, and the few left took a route around his apple cheeks as his burgeoning smile evolved into a full chuckle.

"In life," I began, "you will find that courage is the most important quality to have. As I firefighter, when I show up on my truck and see a house fully on fire I would be a fool not to be afraid to go in, but then I realize that there are people in that house that need me. I have been trained, I have protection, and I took an oath to do my best under every circumstance to separate people from danger. So, I take a deep breath, grab the hose and run into the front door full of fear, but shielded by the courage I need to get the job done." Ronald looked into my eyes, his were no longer glazed over with tears. "You're afraid when you go into a burning building? I thought firefighters were never afraid of anything." I smiled "What do you think, I'm stupid? Only a stupid guy wouldn't be afraid going into a burning building, but that's my job, and I summon up enough courage to get me by. I always try to keep a little courage in me in case I have to do something really scary." Ronald looked down, "I don't think I could ever be a firefighter, I don't have any courage." "Well then," I stated, "it's time we build some. We can do it together because I'm running a little low on it myself." Ronald, quizzically, "How do we do that?" I jumped up onto my feet, stood up straight. "Stand up, Ronald. Stand straight and firm so that nobody can push you down no matter how hard they try." The little man jumped out of bed, stood on his feet, with a resolve as rigid as a steel beam. I put my hand on his shoulder and slightly pushed to find as an immovable force that someone his age could possibly muster.

"Now, take a deep breath in through your nose, hold it down in your chest, and blow it out your mouth." I ordered. As if he was a well drilled soldier, Ronald followed orders precisely. "I feel better!" he announced. "Great, hop up on that stretcher and let's go!" I responded, and so he did. We covered him up, buckled him in and sang a cadence as we marched out of the pediatric emergency department. When they saw us leaving, the nurses came over and hugged the reclining little soldier as we made our way out of the hospital.

Once in the ambulance a feeling of relaxation seemed to envelope the boy. For the first time he looked actually comfortable. We had a little small talk for the beginning of the ride, then I mentioned the braces on his teeth. Ronald explained how he had to have four baby teeth pulled because they would not come out on their own. "You must have got some good money from the tooth fairy for four teeth" I stated. "There's no tooth fairy, just like there is no Santa Claus" was his response. "Now wait just one minute, my friend. I know for a fact there is a Santa Claus." I chided. "My mom told me when I was seven that Santa Claus wasn't real," Ronald replied. Because it was a long ride, I had the opportunity to tell Ronald a story that is very dear to my heart that involved three generations of my family, some selfish people, and a number of people showing the goodness and generosity of human decency. The story ends with the words "So, Santa might not always have a red suit, or a white beard, or might not even be a man; but as long as people truly care for each other and love is in their heart, even if it's only for this one special day, then I can say to you, without a doubt, that Santa Claus is as real as you and me." I told Ronald that I had written this story, and anyone who reads it can't help but cry. He smiled back at me, "I like it too" he said. "So, now do you believe?" I questioned. "Oh, I don't know, I guess so," Ronald replied with a sound of placation in his voice.

The ambulance began to go up a hill, one that I recognized from many trips before. It was the hill leading into the parking lot of the Children's Home. Once the truck took a sharp right turn, I knew we had arrived. "Alright Ronald, take a deep breath through your nose, hold it and blow it all out your mouth," I commanded. The truck came to a complete halt, and Al exited the driver's seat to notify the facility of our arrival. Ronald did what I had requested, and to be honest with you, I did the same because I needed the additional courage to get through this as well.

Suddenly the back doors of the ambulance opened with a jolt and the bright sun shone in, causing both of us to shield our eyes. "Okay Buddy," shouted Al, "we're here." Ronald looked into my eyes with uncertainty. It was time for me to be strong, a rock in a stormy sea. I nodded to him, he nodded back as I began to unbuckle the restraints that secured him to the stretcher. As he swung his legs off the stretcher, he again took a deep breath in through his nose, held it, and blew it out his mouth. Looking up at me with a little more determination, he stood on his feet, grabbed the handle on the back door and jumped out with the mettle of a paratrooper. I took his large bag of belongings and carried them in for him. Ronald and Courage resolutely walked beside me into the Home. As we entered the vestibule, Ronald stopped, looked at me and asked, "Is my mom here?" I had no clue what his mother looked like. There were a number of women inside already, but was one of them Ronald's mom? "I certainly hope so." I replied in full honesty as I hoped with all my heart that she would be there with remorse, reconsidering her decision. Once in the office, all hopes were dashed as she had not yet arrived, she hadn't even called the facility after the initial contact. It was now 11:30. His mother told the nurses that she would be there at 11:00. We asked the chief administrator if we could wait until his mom came to see him. She told us that it was not their regular procedure, but she would allow it. By 12:30 it was obvious to all that there was no reconsideration, there would be no reunion. Ronald had been abandoned.

The administrator, a very warm and kind woman, approached the three of us. As she got closer my mouth went dry and a lump began to form in the back of my throat. "I'm sorry, but we have to go," explained the administrator. Ronald looked up into my eyes, and together we both took a deep breath though our noses, held it, and blew it out. Ronald simultaneously stood up with me, turned to me and shook my hand. His eyes were full of tears, but he had the strength to hold them at their place of origin, not letting them flow down his face. At this point I was so happy that I wore glasses, hoping that he would not be able to see that my eyes were as full of tears as his, and I was not confident that I had the strength to hold them back. "You take care of yourself and Courage, Ronald. It has been an honor and a pleasure meeting you," I stated as we shook hands. "And remember, if you believe he's real, then he's real." Ronald dropped my hand and hugged me around my waist. Without saying a word, Ronald released me from his embrace, took the hand of the administrator and walked down a long corridor. I watched him, but he did not look back.

***

"Al, can you drive back please?" I asked knowing that Al hates driving. He looked at me, nodded his head and said "Ya, get in, I'll drive." Al, a short, stocky fifty year old man with a shaved head knew the feelings that I was experiencing. For a number of years, he and his wife had temporarily housed foster children of different ages. "You can't let yourself get emotionally attached to these cases," Al instructed. "You have to disconnect yourself or else you will burn yourself out." Having been a firefighter for close to thirty years, and an EMT for twenty-five, I was well aware of Al's admonition, and usually abided by it, but this one got to me.

As the day passed, my mind was fixated on this poor kid. I could not help imagining his feeling of abandonment by his mother, being alone in a strange place with strange people at his age. He must have been terrified. Finally, at four o'clock I could no longer help myself. I called the Children's Home, explained who I was, and asked how Ronald was doing. The administrator told me that due to HIPPA laws, she could not give me any information about Ronald; however, she asked me if I was interested in hearing about a young boy that had just checked in, but she couldn't tell me his name. "I would love to hear how one of your boys is doing," I responded. "Well," she began, "He was brought to his room and met his roommate. He is obviously saddened by the whole experience and has asked for his mom a number of times. Unfortunately she has neither showed nor called." My heart sank in my chest. Taking a deep breath I asked her if it would be alright if someone was to bring in a bunch of gifts for Christmas for a certain boy. "We do take donations," she responded. I explained, "This would not be a donation in the regular sense. I would like these gifts to go specifically to a certain child there." There was silence on the phone for a few moments. "Well, you can bring gifts in. Hopefully, I will be in touch with that certain person's parent, and will ask her. If I can't get in touch with her, I don't see any problem with you donating gifts to a specific child, as long as there is no objection." I thanked the woman and for the first time that day felt unburdened in both soul and spirit.

My wife Nancy and I arrived home at the same time that day. We got out of our cars, and she asked how my day was, not knowing the heartbreak that she was about to experience. We sat on the living room couch where I related the events of the day to her. Nancy, after being married to me for twenty-seven years, could sense my emotional status. By the time I had finished telling her the story, she already knew what I was going to say. "So, when do you want to go shopping for him?" I laughed, she knew me better than I knew myself. I was planning to ask her for just that when I finished telling the tale.

"I just want to give this a week or so before I do anything," I explained. "They are going to try to get in touch with his mother. I don't expect any problems; actually I don't expect them to be able to reach her." It would later be proven that my assertion was correct. She neither called nor could they get in touch with her, and I was given permission to bring Ronald gifts. There was, however one catch: I would only be able to drop the packages off in the administration building, as I could have no contact whatsoever with Ronald. In addition, he could not know who the packages came from. I accepted the provisions as stated, notified my wife, and we made a date to go out for dinner and shopping on Friday night.

After a dinner that we both rushed through, Nancy and I went to the mall. We took a shopping cart from the long string of carriages to the toy section. After ten minutes of shopping and having filled the first carriage, we returned to the front of the store to fetch another shopping cart, this time for clothes. By the time we were finished, this little boy would want for nothing. Nancy even picked out a pair of dress pants, shoes, shirt, tie and sweater for Ronald to wear on Christmas day.

For the next two weeks we wrapped the pile of gifts that we had purchased for Ronald. This experience, having pulled my heartstrings down to my knees, caused me to reach out on Facebook where a number of my friends responded to ask how they could help. By the time I was ready to go to the Children's Home, my son Mark and I filled the back of my full size pickup truck to capacity with toys, games, treats and clothing, not only for Ronald, but for many other children as well. Upon my return to the Children's Home, Mark and I began to transfer the contents of my truck into the facility. After a dozen or so trips, by each of us, my truck was finally empty, and the welcoming area of the Children's Home was bursting with gifts. To ensure Ronald's gifts were put aside, on the bright colored wrapping paper we wrote in black magic marker "To Ronald, From Santa Claus." The staff at the Children's Home was dumfounded as they could not believe their eyes. Each administrator hugged Mark and me, thanking us with genuine gratitude. We hugged them back, thanked them for all they did for the children, and returned to my truck for a very pleasant ride home.

***

On the morning of December 28 my phone rang at about 9:30. I read the screen and was excited to see that it was from my contact person at the Children's Home. "Merry Christmas, Susan!" was my greeting. "Hi Bill," replied Susan. "Merry Christmas to you as well. Can I tell you a story?" With a smile on my face that reached from ear to ear I responded with one word, "Absolutely!" Susan began, "On Christmas morning all the children here were woken by the sound of jingle bells ringing down the hallways. As they made their way down to the dining room they found three large piles of colorfully wrapped gifts with signs saying "BOYS," "GIRLS," and "EVERYONE" positioned over their respective piles. The children were instructed to take two gifts each from the piles. The children were shouting with excitement as they ran to the piles to be the first to choose. Each child ran to the back of the room after receiving their gifts. They then sat on the floor tore off the wrappings and opened them. When everyone had opened all their gifts, the children were instructed to go back to their rooms, wash up and ready themselves for breakfast. As they filed out of the room, I separated this one boy from the rest. He asked if he had done something wrong, and I told him no, I wanted him to come with me. We walked down to the staff lunch room where we had piled all the gifts that you had brought. The boy and I walked into the room, he looked at the gifts and asked if I wanted him to bring all the gifts down to the dining room for the other kids. I laughed and told him no, Santa Claus came late last night and left all these gifts here just for you. The boy walked over to the pile and saw his own name and Santa's name prominently displayed on the front of every package. After pausing to comprehend the situation, he turned towards me and exclaimed, 'He is real!'"

No gift, regardless of the size, expense, or rarity can ever compare to the love between a child and a parent. When that bond is removed, there is nothing that can replace it. If a parent passes away, in time there is closure; however, if a parent abandons their child, especially a child who is old enough to realize what is happening, the child will forever wonder why he or she wasn't good enough to earn their parents love. Ronald was a special boy. A strong, courageous boy. By law I could never check in on him with any definitive response other than generalities. I visited the Children's Home a few more times after Christmas with gifts for Ronald, but the newer administrative staff was not as accommodating as Susan was. I guess for the safety of the children this is the best policy, no matter how hard it is to accept.

The next time you are worrying about getting just the right gift for someone, stop for a minute and think about this person — how much you love them, why you love them, and how much they mean to you. Sit down and put these thoughts on paper, wrap it up with a special bow, and place it in their stocking. No gift will ever mean more or be more valuable than your love.

CHAPTER 5

2015

As she slept peacefully in her bed, I knelt down beside her and took her hand. It was warm, soft and frail so I held it gently in mine. Her breaths were fast and shallow, her eyes were closed and my presence did not awaken her. "Mom," I whispered softly. Although she made no acknowledgement to my voice I continued to talk to her with the hope that in some way my words were reaching their intended target. "Sleep Mom, relax, don't fight the rest, welcome it. I want to thank you for everything you and Dad did for me. I am the luckiest person in the world to have such wonderful parents. None of us ever needed for anything. You and Dad did without to make sure that we never had to, and I appreciate it with all my heart. I'm also sorry mom, sorry for any heartache that I ever caused you, for the times I did things that made you angry, or sad, and for all the things I did that may have disappointed you. Sleep now Mom, I love you." I noticed on the alarm clock that it was getting late, and I had to be at work in twenty minutes. I kissed the hand which I was holding, then kissed her cheek and forehead. I turned and said, "God bless you," before I left to go to the fire station for work that night.

Although I am not a religious person, I do consider myself very spiritual Personally, I hear God in an ocean wave hitting the shoreline; in the wind blowing through the trees; in the cry of a baby. I see God in the grain of a piece of wood, a scarlet sky at sunset, or a child playing with a puppy more than I do hearing someone read it to me out of a book.

As I left her bedroom, I approached my sister who told me how good she had done that day. She had sat up at the table, ate some lunch, talked and laughed about old times just before I got there. I asked her if there was anything she needed before I left, and hearing that she didn't, I asked her to call me if she needed anything or if something happened. I kissed her goodnight and went to work.

***

The loud voice could be heard for ten seconds before she appeared around the corner. Her constant protests of being forcibly taken against her will to the hospital by ambulance were expelled vociferously. Her complaints were now heard by almost everyone in the emergency department. The two EMTs dragged her stretcher from the hallway into the ward through the double doorway. Having worked with one of the EMTs at a previous employ, I could tell she was not her usual jovial self. They brought the woman into an empty room and transferred her onto the hospital bed. Throughout this whole procedure her shouting never ceased, and continued after they left the room. The loud rants were reaching the ears of the patients in adjoining rooms and corridors. Although the nurse in charge sat with this woman and tried to discuss the situation, none of her justifications were heard or acknowledged by the woman as she continued her tirade.

After numerous failed attempts to quiet this woman, the nurse walked out of the room and returned to her position on the desk. The nurse's aide inquired what was wrong in room

24. The nurse explained, "She was brought in for trying to hurt herself." Now this being just two days before Christmas, people succumbing to depression and attempting to end their lives is not unusual. However, these people are usually younger to middle aged people. To see a woman of ninety years attempt such an act is quite unusual. "The medics reported that the woman had a bag over her head when the attendant went in her room," continued the nurse. "She just got out of the hospital two weeks ago for abdominal pain, but all the tests were negative."

The incessant shouting became increasingly louder as the woman continued to demand her immediate release. It was evident that a number of the other patients in the ward were getting anxious from the woman's lament. This ward, being the area that temporarily houses patients with psychological emergencies until they can find proper placement in a psychological facility, was full of both anxious and severely depressed patients awaiting transport. With a dozen or so patients already agitated enough to be brought to the hospital, the screams of an elderly woman was enough to counteract the sedating medications that they were given earlier.

Being an EMT, and not having any advanced formal education or training in social work or psychological intervention, my ability to deal with disruptive psych patients should be at best limited, but for some reason or another I have always had the ability to defuse patients with such symptoms. It wasn't long before the complaints began to come in from the other patients in the ward about the continued yelling coming from room 24. Even closing the door to the room offered little relief from the noise. As the nurses and their aides rushed from patient to patient to settle them down, I took it upon myself to try and offer some sense of tranquility to the situation. I knocked on the door and slowly opened it. In the railed bed laid a white haired woman, her face red with unremitting rage. "Who are you? A doctor?" she questioned? "No, I'm Bill, an EMT who works for the hospital." I replied. "May I sit down for a couple of minutes?" I slowly made my way into the room as I spoke and closed the door behind me. "Do whatever you want," growled the woman. "You have no right to keep me here, I want to get out of here!" Her state of agitation was unrelenting. I sat down in the chair next to her, leaned over and rested my arms on the rail of her bed. "What's your name?" I asked.

The woman, for the first time became silent, and began to look me over. I was unsure if she was sizing me up or just preparing for another verbal barrage. "My name is Marion, and I shouldn't be here," she replied, in a terse voice, but with substantially less decibels. "That's terrible. How did you get here?" I asked, already knowing the circumstances of her case. The woman began her vocal assault again, using choppy, yet very precise sentences: "Those bastards brought me here. I was fine. I'm not sick. I don't want any tests. I just got out of here. I'm 90 years old. Don't I have any rights?" At that point I surmised that the woman was more afraid than she was angry. "Well, I don't know why you're here, you sound perfectly fine to me," I answered. "I am fine, now get me out of here!" ordered Marion.

Psychological ailments are not always as they seem, as there are a number of underlying medical reasons that can cause someone to have an altered mental status. People experiencing diabetic reactions, urinary tract infections, concussions, reactions to medications and more, often display symptoms similar to those of irrational psychological behavior. Marion's past medical history allowed us to rule out a number of possible medical reasons, and a blood test would help us to rule out many more. However, Marion was adamantly opposed to any testing, whatsoever. So to rule out some other possibilities, I began to ask Marion a series of very easily answered questions to which she answered immediately, correctly, and gave both colorful as well as off color responses. For having reached the age of ninety, this woman still had a lot on the ball. There was no need to go on with this examination.

I rested my head atop my folded forearms which were already placed comfortably on the rails of Marion's bed. "So Marion, where were you born?" I asked in the most soothing of voices that I could offer. The question must have caught her off guard, as she answered in a more rational tone, "Somerville." I was beginning to calm the once turbulent waters. "I met my wife in Somerville," I responded. "She lived in Porter Square before they did it all over." She nodded her head with acknowledgement. "I'm from Inman Square area originally, before we moved to Scituate. My husband was a Somerville cop, and his name was Bill too." She was opening up to me, slowly, but at this point I would have been satisfied with a nod and smile. "God bless him, I know how hard that job can be. I'm a Quincy Firefighter. I just work at the hospital part time," I informed her. Marion lifted her head, took my hand in hers, and looked directly into my eyes and stated "Firefighters help people. If you're really a firefighter you will help get me out of here. Please, please help get me out of here. I don't want any tests. I don't want any treatment. I still have rights, don't I? Please, no more tests. Don't let them give me any more tests." The urgency in her voice was intense. Marion knew exactly what she wanted, and exactly what she didn't want.

Having already discussed Marion's case with the charge nurse, I was cognizant of the fact that unless otherwise directed by a physician, neither tests nor treatment would be administered to Marion. She had made her wishes known by completing a Do Not Resuscitate order previous to her current situation, which, by law, we have to honor. "Marion," I said softly, "I can promise you that unless a doctor comes into this room and orders tests, no tests or treatment will be performed on you, other than checking your blood pressure and taking a little blood for testing. But you have those things done all the time, so they won't be that bad." Marion, still looking directly into my eyes, this time with obvious fright. The demanding tone of her voice was gone. Now she began to plead, "Don't let them do any tests. Don't lie to me. I don't want any tests. You're a firefighter, you have to help me." I put my free hand atop of hers, and with utmost sincerity, I assured her that no tests and no treatments would be forthcoming unless ordered directly by a doctor. "What did your husband do after he left the Somerville Police Department?" I asked in an attempt to break the tension.

"My husband died fifty years ago, my son died twenty years ago and my daughter died three years ago. My grandchildren live in Colorado and Florida. I have no one, no one but my friends in my knitting club, and they're dying too. Why can't I just go? Why can't my heart just stop beating?" This poor woman had not only experienced the passing of her husband, but countless friends, and two children. Life gives no reason why things happen, nor offers any assistance to withstand their effects. As humans we are just like fish swimming through the ocean of life, having to adjust to whatever changes of tide, temperature or predator which may happen to befall us.

"Bill, please, please tell me they are not going to do any tests on me. Don't let them do any tests on me." A lump was beginning to form in my throat as my thoughts traveled back to a few months ago to my mother. She had spent most of her adult life taking care of her siblings, parents and husband during their long, arduous illnesses. Imagining the profound loss she felt as she watched each one of them pass away despite all the love and care which she so unselfishly provided. When finally her work was complete and she could enjoy the things in life she so loved, it was her health that began to fail. She became less and less able to perform the tasks that she previously never considered strenuous. No longer could she travel abroad, cook the impressive meals she loved to make, shop for new clothes, or attend nights out with friends. Her excursions had become short trips to and from a variety of physician's offices and hospitals. No longer could she enjoy the aroma of an autumn day or the air after a summer shower, as now her sense of smell was corrupted by the continuous flow of bottled oxygen by way of a nasal cannula.

Sensing her own mortality, she admitted that she was tired, and welcomed an ending to her long journey. She was not afraid, and she was not sad. She wanted us to know that she was tired, and ready to go onto whatever it is that awaits us. After a day surrounded by family and friends where she shared stories and laughter, she went to bed. As she slept, we shared our last moment together.

The next morning I received a call after working overnight at the fire station. It was a call that brought with it a number of emotions, expectation, dread, relief and sadness. As my brother laid in the twin bed beside hers, my mother's night was anything but restful. She moaned, cried and called out throughout the night, and my brother tended to her every need. When morning came she finally fell into a restful sleep. Being awake all night, my brother laid his head onto the pillow and closed his eyes for a moment. When my sister heard silence coming from the bedroom, she walked in and found that my mother had passed in her sleep, holding off death long enough to allow my brother to not have to witness her last breath.

I was sad that I was not there to escort my mother into her next life, to calm her fears, to hold her hand. Not being there when she needed me most has haunted me since that day. This was not a thing for which I could atone, and I would have to live with this self-resentment for the rest of my life.

**

The door slowly opened as a nurse's aide and phlebotomist entered. "We need to get your blood pressure and a vial of blood from you Marion," The aide informed the old woman. Her statement was immediately met with protest. "No, no tests, I don't want any tests, I don't want to be treated. Don't touch me!" ordered Marion. The aide began to argue with the woman with no success. Marion was determined not to have anything done to her. I asked the aide to hold off for a minute and began to explain the situation to Marion. "Marion, do you know what the most important thing a hospital does? It's not what you may think it is. A hospital has to make money to be able to offer care. If we don't follow all the rules and regulations of Medicare, Medicare will deny payment. Now Medicare requires a baseline blood pressure, pulse, oxygen level and temperature, and we have to take a blood test to rule out any infection. That's it." Marion paused, took a breath, and asked, "Do you promise me that this is all they are going to do? No other tests. Do you promise... as a firefighter?" I nodded my head and again promised her, "Unless a doctor overrules us, there will be no additional tests, I promise." Marion looked at the aid and phlebotomist, shook her head, announced her acquiescence to their requests and let them perform their assigned duties.

Although her blood pressure was good, her pulse was racing, most likely from hours of agitation and fear. The aide told her that since her pulse was high she would have to take an EKG, to which the protests once again commenced. "Is that really necessary?" I interrupted as the two ladies argued over the more invasive test. "She is in an agitated state. A pulse of ninety-six is not that high if someone is excited. Since her blood pressure is within normal limits, I think she will be okay. Marion, who had stopped talking while I spoke, was looking up at me as I spoke. It was the longest time that she had been quiet since she had been in the hospital. The aide looked at me with both a little anger and question in her eyes. Protocol would dictate that an elevated pulse on a patient mandated an EKG; who was I to overrule hospital protocols? "Can I see you outside for a minute?" I said to the aide. The phlebotomist was finishing drawing blood from Marion's arm as the aide and I exited her room. "I'm sorry," I said. "I thought you were aware of the situation. This woman has a Do Not Resuscitate order which calls for comfort care measures only. We don't need to monitor her vitals, I already cleared it with the charge nurse. If a doctor orders us, it's a different story, but right now we are just going to stay status." The aide shrugged her shoulders, said okay, and went into room 24 to retrieve her equipment. When the aide and phlebotomist exited the room, I re-entered.

Marion stared into my eyes, "You did this for me? You stopped them from doing tests on me?" Nodding my head, I answered, "I made a promise to you, didn't I? Unless a doctor overrules it, you will have no more tests." Marion reached out and took my hand in hers. "Bill, you are an angel, an angel here on earth. Thank you, thank you so much." Color began to return to her chalk-like complexion and her eyes were filled with tears. "Thank you God, thank you for answering my prayers, no more tests."

"Marion, I did not do anything, but you did the last time you were here; you signed the order that you wanted no more tests or treatments," I responded. She closed her eyes and began to rest, still holding my hand. As I began to whisper to her, telling her to rest, thoughts of my mother, of those last few moments I spent with her flooded my memory. I stopped whispering and instead took a few deep breaths. Marion opened her eyes, looked at me and asked, "Bill, my heart is not in very good condition, why doesn't it just stop and let me rest? I'm tired, I don't have anyone anymore, all my friends and family are gone. Why doesn't my heart just stop beating." Her words cut through me like a sharp scissors through tissue paper. The lump that had begun to form earlier now felt like a golf ball in my throat. Once again I was standing at the doorway between life and death with someone who wanted only to rest.

"Marion, there is a reason that everyone is here on this earth. We each have a job to do here." As I said before, I am not a religious person, but I do consider myself very spiritual, and I thought sharing my beliefs might, in some way, relax this frightened woman. I continued, "We don't know what it is, often we don't even know if we fulfilled our duty, but we can't leave here without completing it."

"What can I do? What was my job? If I haven't done it yet, it's not going to get done," responded Marion. Sometimes moments occur when you forget your place, and instead of separating yourself from a situation like you should, you instead jump right into it with both feet. "Marion, I don't know what my job is either, but wouldn't it be funny if our fates collided and both of us are here, now fulfilling both of our duties?" Marion's look of determination turned quizzical. "What are you talking about?" she questioned.

I took a deep breath, blew it out my mouth and started my explanation. I began by telling her the story of my mother's passing, and how I was not there at her last moments. I told her how much I regretted it and wished with all my heart that I could have held her hand to help her. It was then that I took it to the next step; "So Marion, maybe I am here to help you relax, protect you and stop anything you don't want happening to you. And maybe you are here as an emissary of my mother, to let me help someone at the moment she needed someone most. Maybe, just maybe, we are a Christmas gift to each other." Marion looked into my eyes with a look that I had not seen in her before. She placed her other hand on top of mine and said, "Thank you Bill, merry Christmas."

A knock on the door broke the tension that we had created and a tall man with dark skin, wearing a long white lab coat and glasses walked into the room. "Hello Marion!" said the man with an unmistakable African accent. "I am Doctor Andele. How are you feeling?" Rather than answer him directly, Marion looked at me for advice. I smiled and told her talk to the doctor. Marion began to once again tell the story that I had already heard twice that night. When she finished with the facts, she once again began to plea, "Please doctor, no tests. I don't want any tests or any treatment. I have rights, I signed something a while ago saying this." Dr. Andele smiled, put his hand on her shoulder and reassured her, "No Marion, there will be no more tests. You don't need any, you seem fine to me. I am just going to make arrangements to send you back to the nursing home. But I want you to promise me that you will rest, and will take care of yourself, okay?" Marion swore that she would be fine and would do what he asked of her. As the doctor left the room, Marion called out to him, "Merry Christmas doctor." The doctor turned and smiled. "It will be about an hour or so before your ride is here, but you're going home. Happy holidays," he wished her as the door closed behind him.

"Now, see how all that worrying was for nothing?" I asked. "You got yourself all upset, and now you're just going home." Marion again took my hand in hers and said, "Thank you Bill. You are an angel. You saved my life." I laughed, "Marion, I did not save your life, and I am certain that in no way am I an angel. I'm just happy that our paths crossed tonight." Marion began to shake her head side to side, saying, "It wasn't our paths that crossed. It was our fates." I nodded my head, believing that she might be exactly right. "Maybe," I said. "Now I have to get back to work over at the nurses station. It's time for you to rest. Close your eyes and rest, I will turn out the light and the ambulance will be here before you know it." With that, Marion lifted herself off the bed, and put her arms around me, giving me a big hug. "Merry Christmas Bill, merry Christmas to your whole family. And thank you so much. You might not be God's angel, but you're mine." I hugged her back, helped her get comfortable in the bed, kissed her forehead and left the room.

Sitting back at the nurse's station, I watched Marion on the monitor. She was finally at rest and sleeping soundly. I watched intermittently to insure her chest rose and fell from breathing. She was quiet, the ward was quiet, and all was well.

At 11:00 my shift ended. I packed up my belongings, put my coat on and left the nurses station. As I walked by room 24 I peered in to see Marion still fast asleep. I smiled and said in a soft voice so not to wake her, "Good night Marion, merry Christmas, and thank you." As I walked out of the hospital I had a feeling of inner peace that I had not felt since before my mother had died. I may not be a religious person, but I know there is something out there. After all, something had to make the gasses that created the Big Bang. Call it happenstance, call it coincidence, or call it fate, deep down inside I knew my mother was using this woman as her conduit to let me know she was alright. I walked to my car, catching the occasional snowflake on my nose as it fell from the dark night sky. As I got into my truck, I closed the door and breathed a breath that I had been holding for nine months.

EPILOGUE

It is not just at Christmas that people need help, whether it be physical, emotional or financial. As even the brightest skies have clouds, there are those around us who even in the best of times are in need of assistance. However, the silver lining around these clouds is the love, compassion and generosity that is provided by those who are willing to offer a part of themselves to bring happiness to others. Ultimately, the very act of committing yourself to assist the less fortunate will create a level of oneness and serenity that no other experience can provide. Nevertheless, it is still very true that the greatest of riches are those amassed by selflessly giving of yourself to others than those riches that are achieved just by receiving. Once you feel the uplifting reaction which accompanies this deed, you will surely realize that the gift is truly in the giving.

I wish you all health, happiness and love throughout the year.

ABOUT THE AUTHOR

My name is Bill Arienti. I am a husband, father and firefighter for over 32 years; all three of which I am proud. As a child, my father (also a firefighter) instilled in me the belief that those who have been given much in life owe a debt to those whom fortune has been less kind.

It is through these lessons that I learned how helping others brings more happiness and satisfaction than acquiring material goods ourselves.

If you believe in the message of this book, please leave a review to help others find it.

42271589R00060

Made in the USA
San Bernardino, CA
02 December 2016